Secrets of Wimbledon Common
and Putney Heath

by
Clive Whichelow

Published by

Enigma Publishing
4 Charnwood Avenue
London SW19 3EJ
www.enigmapublishing.co.uk

First edition May 2000

ISBN 0 9524297 6 4

By the same author:
Mysterious Wimbledon (with Ruth Murphy) ISBN 0 9524297 0 5
More Mysterious Wimbledon (with Ruth Murphy) ISBN 0 9524297 5 6
Pubs of Wimbledon Village (Past & Present) ISBN 0 9524297 1 3

Printed by Roebuck Press

CONTENTS

INTRODUCTION

On the surface the Common is a pleasant place to walk, a green oasis in the suburban sprawl between Putney and Wimbledon. But what secrets does it hold?

The answer is surprisingly many. We all know the windmill, the Common's main landmark, but there was another windmill nearby over two hundred years before the present one was built, and the miller was horrifically murdered there.

And how many people realise that John Constable, England's most celebrated landscape artist worked here, completing several sketches and paintings locally?

Through the centuries the Common has been a favourite haunt of other artists and writers too, who have been attracted by the peace and tranquillity to be found here. It has also been visited by kings and queens, and has been the venue for duels, prize-fights, and mock battles. The Common is also haunted by many ghosts, both actual and metaphorical.

And where do the evocative names come from? Beverley Brook, Queensmere, Robin Hood ride... all have a story to tell.

Books about the Common have been written before but this one attempts to uncover some little-known facts about it, and expand on some of the stories which have been barely touched upon in the past.

So, whether you are reading this at home or taking it with you as you walk the ancient pathways, prepare to discover some of the secrets of Wimbledon Common.

Why is there a Robin Hood Ride on the Common? Surely Robin Hood never rode near here? Sadly not, but the path used to lead to the inn of this name at Kingston Vale, and the name has stuck ever since. Caesar's Well was also known previously as Robin Hood Well.

BEATING THE BOUNDS

It seems ironic that in centuries gone by the dividing line between Wimbledon Common and Putney Heath was the subject of fierce dispute, but today few people either know or care where the boundary lies.

Beating the bounds is an ancient custom, still retained in some parts, of locals led by the churchwardens going round the parish boundaries, usually on Ascension Day, and beating against them with sticks. Often, the children were lightly beaten too so they would remember where the boundaries were and inhabitants of neighbouring parishes were bumped against the boundary stones for the same reason. Future disputes could then be settled by those thus initiated. At the end of the beating session a Church Ale would often be held and the children would be rewarded with pennies. The practice is believed to have evolved from the Roman feast of Terminialia when offerings were made to the god of landmarks, Terminus.

The first recorded beating of the bounds locally was in 1655 when a Wimbledon court decided that the perambulation should take place 'before Midsomer Day next... betwixt this manor of Wymbledon and Wandsworth.' It was also agreed that the Lord of the manor of Wandsworth would be informed so that he and his tenants may also attend.

The present day boundary between Wimbledon and Putney, which was finally fixed in 1846 after much dispute between the parishes, runs south-westerly from opposite Queensmere Road on Parkside to just south of Gravelly Ride at Beverley Brook. So while the windmill is on Wimbledon Common (just), Queensmere is on Putney Heath. Some of the boundary stones can still be seen today; for example, just north of the windmill, and at Beverley Brook.

Even though the boundary had been fixed in 1846 the beating of the bounds continued for another half a century. The last recorded perambulation was on May 19th 1898 (Ascension Day). It seems also to have been more than just a ceremonial duty as the vestry clerk and the borough engineer were afterwards each awarded two guineas compensation for extensive damage to their clothes.

For the purposes of this book Wimbledon Common and Putney Heath have been regarded as an entity, and Coombe Wood as an extension of them both in past centuries. The Coombe Neville land was only separated from the Common by Beverley Brook in the last century, and in the 18th century the Coombe, or Comb land extended as far north as the present Putney Vale cemetery, so the history of the three areas is inextricably intertwined. In some cases, notably duelling and prize-fighting, exact locations for events have almost certainly been confused, and the distinction between Wimbledon Common and Putney Heath or Wimbledon Common and Coombe Wood has not been always made. The disputes over the boundaries and the changing of boundary lines cannot have helped.

JOHN CONSTABLE AT WIMBLEDON & PUTNEY

It may surprise some people to learn that England's most famous landscape painter worked in Wimbledon and Putney, and was familiar with the area for over a quarter of a century.

Born in Suffolk in 1776 he studied art in London from 1795, and exhibited at the Royal Academy every year from 1802. He met his future wife, Maria Bicknell in 1809, and visited Putney when her family stayed there from 1815 onwards. He may also have visited the 'country cottage' that the family had used in Wimbledon the previous year.

However, it seems that Constable knew the area already, for in 1812 he had visited and sketched Coombe Wood. In a letter to Maria dated June 6th 1812 he tells how the previous day he had taken a walk with fellow painter Tom Stothard.

He writes: 'I left my door about six in the morning. We breakfasted at Putney, went over to Wimbledon Common and passed three hours at least in Coombe Wood (Stothard is a butterfly catcher), where we dined by the spring.'

The sketch Constable completed that day is reproduced here. Other Constable work of local scenes survives too. He painted *Houses at Putney Heath* in 1818 (see cover of this book), and a similar, tinted drawing entitled *Bristol House, Putney Heath*. He completed three separate copies of this, and it is thought that he may have intended one each for his wife and her sisters. (Adjoining Bristol House was Louisa Cottage, Maria's family home).

Constable also completed a sketch of the Octagonal House at Putney Heath, which is now in a private collection, and the Admiralty telegraph, also at Putney. In addition to this he made a sketch of Wimbledon Park in 1815. His future wife's family did not approve of the couple's relationship and on the morning of July 3rd he had met her at Putney Bridge and taken her to Wimbledon Park so they could spend time together without her family's disapproval.

In addition to the above, Constable also completed *View Towards London* from Putney and a *View Across a Wood* which is believed to be a local scene. Both of these are in private collections.

It is thought that most of Constable's drawings were made in sketch-books, some of which were very small. Only eight sketch-books are known to have survived in one piece. In one of the small ones is another local drawing, of a cedar tree, inscribed 'Putney Heath 18th November 1819'. Constable also completed a small sketch of the windmill on Wimbledon Common (see next page), though it is unfortunately undated.

There may well be other sketches of local scenes but some of Constable's drawings have generic titles and cannot be easily attributed to specific areas. What is clear though, is that he knew the area before he met his future wife, and visited it many times after her father took the house on Putney Heath.

After the death of Maria's father in March 1828 the family house, Louisa Cottage, was left to Maria's sister after whom it had been named. Later that year, in November, Maria too died. Constable continued to visit the cottage until his own death in 1837.

So it seems that Constable's association with Putney and Wimbledon spanned at least twenty-five years, and there may well be more of his work, albeit sketches, that have yet to be attributed to the area.

CONSTABLE'S SKETCH OF WIMBLEDON WINDMILL (UNDATED)

Another eminent 19th century artist who painted landscapes of Wimbledon Common was William Callow. He painted a watercolour of Wimbledon Common showing the windmill, and another showing what appears to be Westside. Born in Greenwich in 1812, he travelled and painted extensively in Europe throughout his life but was based in London from 1841 to 1855. He died in 1908.

HORSERACING

Think of horseracing in Surrey and you think of Epsom, Goodwood, and others, but Wimbledon too was once a regular venue for the sport of kings. References to meetings on Wimbledon Common and Putney Heath are sparse and elusive, but races were being held here as early as the 17th century. Samuel Pepys records calling on Sir William Coventry in 1667 only to find that he had gone to 'run some horses' on Putney Heath with the King and the Duke of York.

In the following century there were organised race meetings at Wimbledon from 1729 through the 1730s. The races included the annual King's Plate which had also been mentioned in an issue of Read's Weekly Journal dated September 6th 1718. It reported that: 'The King's Plate was won on Thursday night at Wimbleton by Mr Harvey of Comb's horse.' So, despite the gap in the records between 1718 and 1729 it is very possible that the Wimbledon race meetings were being held continuously throughout this period.

Also, in the 19th century, there was a regular Wimbledon, Cheam and Kingston meeting though no specific location has been established. The final meeting was held on March 10th 1862.

All the above were organised meetings, and there were probably many more one-off point-to-point races which have gone unrecorded.

Most people know that Lord Baden-Powell wrote his classic *Scouting For Boys* at the windmill on Wimbledon Common, but how many know of his brother's local claim to fame? On June 30th 1909 Major B. Baden-Powell founded the Kite-Flying Association of Great Britain. Competitions were held regularly on Wimbledon Common, and although the club did not survive the First World War kite flying is still regularly seen in the field by the windmill.

A Horrible Cruel and bloudy Murther,
Committed at Putney in Surrey on the 21. of
Aprill laſt, 1614, *being thurſday, vpon the body*
of Edward Hall *a Miller of the ſame pariſh*,
Done by the hands of *Iohn Selling, Peeter Pet* and *Edward Streater*,
his ſeruants to the ſaid *Hall*, each of them giuing
him a deadly blow (as he lay ſleeping)
with a Pickax.

Publiſhed by Authority.

Imprinted at London for *Iohn Wright*, and are to be ſold without Newgate
at the ſigne of the Bible. 1614.

THE OTHER WINDMILL

The windmill is probably the single best-known of the landmarks on the Common, but how many people realise that there was once another windmill nearby over two hundred years before the present one was built in 1817, or that the miller was horrifically murdered there?

The open-trestle post mill stood at Windmill Corner, which is now known as Tibbet's Corner, and was erected in 1613 – perhaps an unlucky date for the miller.

On April 21st 1614, the miller, Edward Hall, was murdered by three of his servants; Peter Pet, John Selling, and Edward Streater. They bludgeoned him with a pickaxe as he lay sleeping. His crime? In the words of the pamphlet sold outside Newgate prison, describing the murder: 'his natural inclination was to bee sparing and miserable with his housekeeping, which procured him the hatred of his servants and familie'.

Hall's wife was pregnant, and in an effort to save himself money and trouble, he sent her off to her mother's in the country. This gave his servants the opportunity they had been waiting for.

On the 21st of April, at about 10 o'clock, just after supper, Hall lay sleeping in the chair by the fire in the kitchen. Pet and Selling, seizing their opportunity, crept up behind the miller and hit him with a pickaxe: Pet with a blow to the back, and Selling to the head. At this point, Streater wasn't even present. He was grinding corn some distance away.

Pet called him to the scene, and with Selling persuaded him to administer a blow with the pickaxe. They then took the body to the stable, dug a hole, and buried it. Next, they took their master's horse, saddled and bridled it, and set it loose in Wimbledon Wood to give the impression that Hall had been attacked there by strangers. They then ransacked the miller's house, taking between £30 and £40.

Within a week however, the miller was missed by his neighbours, and Streater, followed by the others, confessed to the crime.

It is not known what punishment the three were given, or indeed, what became of the miller's wife and child, but the windmill was there for at least another twenty years, and the last recorded mention of it at this site was in 1636. It was later moved by oxen to a site by the Thames at Wandsworth, but seems to have gone by around 1800.

CROMWELL'S WATER-MILL

There was once also a water-mill on the Common, owned, it is said, by Walter Cromwell, father of Thomas, Henry VIII's famous Lord High Chamberlain. Looking at Beverley Brook now it is hard to believe that its modest waters were once strong enough to drive a mill, but this is what it did in the 15th century, and the name Mill Corner remains to remind us of the fact.

Edward Walford asserts in Greater London that there is 'not the slightest doubt' that this fulling mill once belonged to Walter Cromwell. He is supposed to have built it here when the lease on his father's mill on the Wandle expired around 1473-74.

In Fishponds Wood there is still a pond which is believed to have originally belonged to Cromwell's water-mill. According to one account the mill burned down around 1600, but we know that it was still there in 1617 when Ralph Treswell carried out his survey of the manor for Thomas Cecil, the Lord of the Manor.

The mill seems to have gone by the end of the century though as it is not mentioned in a detailed survey of Wimbledon in 1649.

It is thought that the ponds in Fishponds Wood were man-made and that they were specifically created for use with the mill. One can also see that there is a very definite kink in the Beverley Brook at Mill Corner and this may well have been artificially created for milling purposes.

A great deal of mystery surrounds the origins and even the demise of this water-mill, but as so often is the case the name alone is the only part of its history that remains.

The Duel in which William Pitt took part on the Common in 1798 is well-known, but the fact that Pitt survived the encounter has had a profound impact on us all ever since. The year after walking away from the duel in one piece Pitt introduced income tax for the first time. And although intended as a temporary measure to fund the Napoleonic wars, it has been with us ever since. How different things may have been if his opponent, George Tierney had been a better shot!

GHOSTS AND LEGENDS

Wimbledon seems to have more than its fair share of ghosts, so it is no surprise that there have been ghostly sightings on and around the Common.

It is said that anyone brave enough to stand on Putney Heath at midnight on January 30th may see the headless ghost of Charles I galloping by on his horse towards London. He apparently rode the old Portsmouth Road on this date to see his children at Ham House before he was executed in 1649.

The Portsmouth Road would seem to be an ideal area for ghost-hunters with the tales of highwaymen and their victims associated with the area. More than one writer has spoken of the ghost of Jerry Abershaw appearing on the Common – and his ghost has even featured in the novel Lavengro by George Borrow. There have been no recent sightings of the ghost though. Perhaps after two hundred years it is finally at rest.

There have however been very recent reports of hauntings at the Windmill. Occupants of the cottage beneath the windmill (which is now an exhibition area) have reported ghostly footsteps and rattling chains as recently as the 1990s, and one couple who lived in the cottage were so alarmed that they even had the place exorcised.

Another ghost story from the early 20th century concerns the actor Edward Sillward who was walking across the Common one night when he saw a man in convict's clothes running, and then suddenly disappearing. When he told friends about this he was informed that others too had seen the apparition. Perhaps what he had seen was the ghost of an inmate escaping from the 'birdcage' which stood in Church Road until 1896. Or perhaps it was the ghost of local spiritualist and writer W.T. Stead who always wore his prison uniform on the anniversary of his release from prison in January 1886. He had been convicted of child prostitution charges (which he had deliberately sought in order to bring about a change in the law regarding the age of consent).

But some ghost stories must be taken with a bushel or two of salt. One writer has spoken of the ghost of a Roman centurion who wanders near Caesar's Camp. As most locals know, the camp has no connection with Caesar, and there have been very few Roman remains found in the area.

The manor court rolls provide a useful history of events relating to the Common from the 15th century onwards. But in 1499 there is a joke. Many of the entries in the rolls refer to various people being prosecuted for illegally taking wood or furze from the Common, and this entry mentions a Robert Hunt entering the Common and 'unjustly cutting two cartloads of underwood in sapling to the prejudice of the lord'. A note in the margin however reads: 'excused because he is dead.'

A GYPSY CAMP c. 1856

THE GYPSIES' RING

One of the reasons so much of the Common's history has been forgotten is the fact that modern maps do not always show the old landmarks. And so it is with the Gypsies' Ring. The map in Walter Johnson's Wimbledon Common shows it between White Cottage and Caesar's Well. It is also very possible that the gypsies may have used Caesar's Camp which until 1875 had not been levelled and would have made an ideal and secluded spot for their temporary home.

In the 19th century gypsy travellers on their way to Wandsworth Common would stop here every year and set up camp. Surprisingly, they were tolerated, even welcomed, by the local people. Even Charlotte Marryat of the grand Wimbledon House would come out and read the Bible to them on Sunday afternoons. One of the gypsies, Mignonette Lee was converted to Christianity and even attended St. Mary's church in the Village. One writer also speaks of the excitement in the Village when the gypsies came.

The gypsy families that came back to Wimbledon Common year after year were the Lees, the Coopers, and the Smiths. They collected heather on the Common and used it to make brooms to sell to the Villagers.

The gypsies also drew the attention of various well-known writers of the day, such as Theodore Watts-Dunton, Charles Leland, and most notably George Borrow, all of whom wished to learn more of the gypsy way of life. Borrow and Leland both studied and wrote about the Romany language and culture. Watts-Dunton was even known to receive gypsy visitors at his Putney home, the Pines.

It is not known when the gypsies first came to Wimbledon, but they had been known in England since the 16th century when they arrived from the continent. But by the turn of the 20th century they were seen less frequently when the authorities started to clamp down on them and reduce the number of sites available for setting up camp.

When Earl Spencer wanted to enclose the Common in 1864 he cited the gypsies as one of the reasons for taking action. He said: 'Besides being immoral characters, they bring contagious diseases and do not submit to sanitary and other regulations, commit depredations, and in other respects are not desirable neighbours to the houses that are now found near here'. This judgement seems rather at odds with the almost idyllic image of the Romanies being welcomed by the Villagers only a few years previously, but it would have been useful ammunition in the war over the Common's future. So by the early 20th century the gypsies no longer came to Wimbledon Common, but they had left behind them another little piece of Wimbledon history.

One story, perhaps apocryphal, which mentions gypsies on the Common in the early 18th century is that of Daniel Watney. Born in 1705, the first known ancestor of the famous brewing family was said to have been found on Wimbledon Common soon after his birth by a local farmer named Acres. The baby was thought to have been left by gypsies after they moved camp. The farmer and his wife brought the boy up and could not decide on a name for him. Their discussions on what name to call the child are said to have resulted in 'Watney' as a corruption of 'what name'. Daniel Watney married the farmer's daughter, Mary at St. Mary's church on August 23rd 1730.

PRIZE-FIGHTING

Along with Coombe Wood, Coombe Warren and Molesey Hurst, Wimbledon Common was one of the most popular venues for bare-knuckle prize-fighting in the 18th and early 19th centuries.

The sport had been declared illegal in 1750 but continued to flourish, often patronised by the nobility. The Duke of Clarence, later to become King William IV, allowed Bushy Park Estate to be used for prize-fighting bouts. Because of this, fights here and in the surrounding area often had a blind eye turned to them by the authorities.

There were at least seventeen bare-knuckle fights on Wimbledon Common between 1788 and 1823, and many more at neighbouring Coombe Wood and Coombe Warren. In fact, the fights were sometimes moved from one venue to another on the occasions when the authorities did attempt to stop them.

Some of the more notable fights on Wimbledon Common were:

Belcher vs Gamble on December 22nd 1800, Tom Jones vs Elias the Jew (also known as Dutch Sam) on July 15th 1801, and Henry 'Game Chicken' Pearse vs Edward Bourke on January 24th 1804.

The latter match, for a £100 purse, lasted well over an hour and totalled 28 rounds, and was one of the matches moved several times to evade the authorities. The organiser, Thomas Owen, was prosecuted and imprisoned for three months for riot and conspiracy. The Morning Advertiser reported that there was a crowd of 1500 watching the fight, and that Owen, in his defence, said that if he was guilty then so were the noblemen and others in attendance.

A fight at nearby Coombe Warren reported in The News of February 11th 1816 gives a flavour of the rough and ready bouts which took place. The contest, on Tuesday February 6th was between Carter, and 'a black named Joseph'. The purse was 25 guineas – more than a year's wages for an agricultural labourer at the time.

The betting was 2 to 1 on Carter, and the men had two 'seconds' each, indicating that there was at least some semblance of organisation. The fighting itself however included what would now be regarded as foul play. This of course was fifty years before the Queensberry rules were introduced in 1867. The match was reported as follows:

1. Carter got to his length and placed a smart blow on the Black's eye. The Black went in over-handed and his short left and right and a sort of rally followed when first blood was drawn very slightly from Carter's mouth. In a struggle Carter got his adversary's head under his left arm and was punishing him with his right when the Black shewed strength and extricated himself. Both were down but Carter was thrown out of the ring.

2. The Black received the hit again with Carter's left hand. A close took place and Carter was again thrown and shewed bad condition in want of wind. 7 to 4 on Carter.

3. This round shewed that although the Black had strength he was not quick enough in returning the left hand blow, which was again given. Carter broke away after delivering. A smart rally, in which the Black hit his best with much determination. In a close both were down.

4. Although Carter was open-mouthed, his adversary had neither science nor quickness to do any thing. The Black received three or four left hand hits on the head, and some inoffensive ones with the right hand. In a close the Black had Carter's head exchequered, but the latter held his right hand and got down.

5. Much parleying, and Carter blowing like a half-trained horse after a King's plate. He, however, hit and broke away, until the Black in following was knocked down, for the first time, and turning himself into a seat, he looked around as if to find a way out. 7 to 2 on Carter.

6. Equally distressed, the Black made an effectual lunge at Carter's body which partially told. Carter hit, and shewed off much science in stopping; but the Black proved to have superior strength at the end of the round, and threw his adversary.

7. Carter danced about and made one hit, when the Black deliberately looked out for the best place to lay down after he had got on his knees, for it was not the effect of any blow – 10 to 1 on Carter.

8. Carter pushed him down with the right hand.

9. The Black laid hold of Carter's left hand, as he was about to hit. On receiving a blow the Black put his hand to his mouth and deliberately walked away in the Iky Pig style; and moving his hands, as if supplicating for a cessation of hostilities, he said 'stop'. The seconds threw up their hats for victory, and Carter jumped out of the ring; but as the Black did not mean to give in, as it was afterwards found, to it they went again. Twenty six minutes had now elapsed, and we call it the close of a bad fight; but Blackee stood up another eighteen minutes only to receive, for he had no chance of giving. The battle was for a purse of 25 guineas and a stake of 25 guineas a side.

It sounds as though the betting was pretty feverish throughout the bout, with odds changing as it progressed, and it is easy to imagine the passions aroused not just by the fighting itself but by the ebb and flow of money riding on it. There was a second bout that day between a fighter named Ballard and an unnamed Jewish sailor.

Fights on the Common were still being organised as late as 1830 when a match was being planned between William Perry and Barney Dogherty. However, once the authorities got wind of it the venue was switched to Mortlake, only to be changed twice more to avoid prosecution.

Although the bare-knuckle fights came to an end, Wimbledon had played an important part in what was the forerunner to the modern sport of boxing.

THE PICNIC SPOT, WIMBLEDON COMMON

MAYES FARM, 1910

72 T

FARMING ON THE COMMON

A surprising fact about Wimbledon Common is that until well into the 20th century there were several working farms on or at the edge of it.

The name Warren Farm still exists but the building today is a private residence. It was still a working farm until the 1930s and can claim a history at least as far back as 1617 when it was mentioned in a survey of the manor. It was then a rabbit farm as the name suggests, and by the 18th century had been taken over by the Watney family; first David, then his son Matthew. In more recent times it has been owned by Lord Russell of Liverpool, Lord Swaythling, and Lord Hore-Belisha.

Not far from Warren farm, near Caesar's Well, was Mayes Farm* about which little history is known. It was still a working farm until well into the 20th century, and in Edwardian times was often the subject of picture postcards showing the small farmhouse and duck-pond. It was sometimes referred to as the 'picnic spot'.

By the 1930s it was equipped with a launder room which took its water from Caesar's Well and had the wonderful name of The Roman Well Steam Laundry. The laundry was still there as late as 1959, but by then the farm had ceased to exist.

Just at the edge of the Common, at the end of Stag lane where the Asda supermarket now stands was Newlands Farm. It can boast greater antiquity than the other farms on the Common, going back as it does to medieval times. Although the area later reverted to woodland, it was cleared for agricultural use again by the early 17th century. In the 19th century wheat grown here was ground at the windmill on Wimbledon Common.

In 1891 part of Newlands farm was sold off for use as the new Putney Vale Cemetery. Twenty years later much of the remaining farm land was acquired as part of the Common when Richardson Evans was carrying out his Commons extension scheme.

Just over the south-west border of the Common was Robin Hood Farm. This had existed since the 17th century and was still a working farm until 1937. Owners included Lord Thurso and Major W. Fox Pitt.

What is the connection between Wimbledon Common and the Trafalgar Square lions? When the National Rifle Association were based here in the 19th century they had two moving targets: The Running Deer and The Running Man. The Running Deer was designed by Sir Edward Landseer, designer of the lions in Trafalgar Square. Why such a grand personage was enlisted to design an object that was to be blasted full of holes is not known, but perhaps it does illustrate the importance of the NRA at that time. Even The Running Man was designed by no lesser figure than the famous Victorian artist G. F. Watts

---

* William Mayes ran the Union beer house, the predecessor to the Fox & Grapes in Camp Road, in 1860.

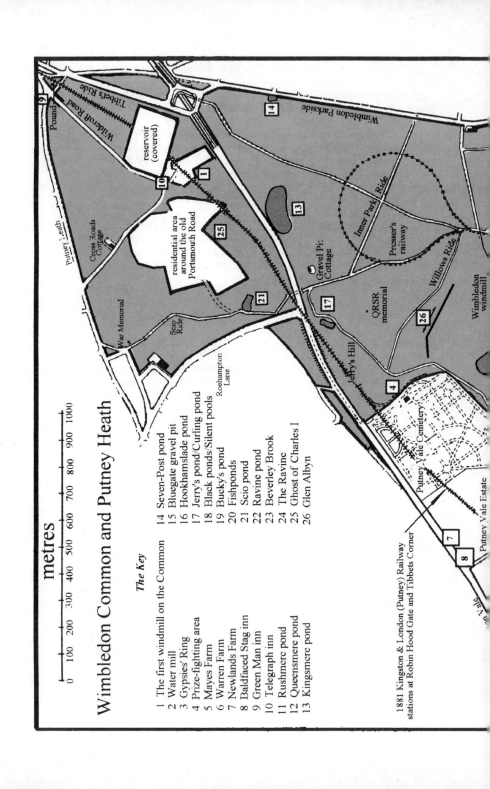

Wimbledon Common and Putney Heath

metres

0   100   200   300   400   500   600   700   800   900   1000

The Key

 1 The first windmill on the Common
 2 Water mill
 3 Gypsies' Ring
 4 Prize-fighting area
 5 Mayes Farm
 6 Warren Farm
 7 Newlands Farm
 8 Baldfaced Stag inn
 9 Green Man inn
10 Telegraph inn
11 Rushmere pond
12 Queensmere pond
13 Kingsmere pond

14 Seven-Post pond
15 Bluegate gravel pit
16 Hookhamslade pond
17 Jerry's pond/Curling pond
18 Black ponds/Silent pools
19 Bucky's pond
20 Fishponds
21 Scio pond
22 Ravine pond
23 Beverley Brook
24 The Ravine
25 Ghost of Charles I
26 Glen Albyn

1881 Kingston & London (Putney) Railway
stations at Robin Hood Gate and Tibbets Corner

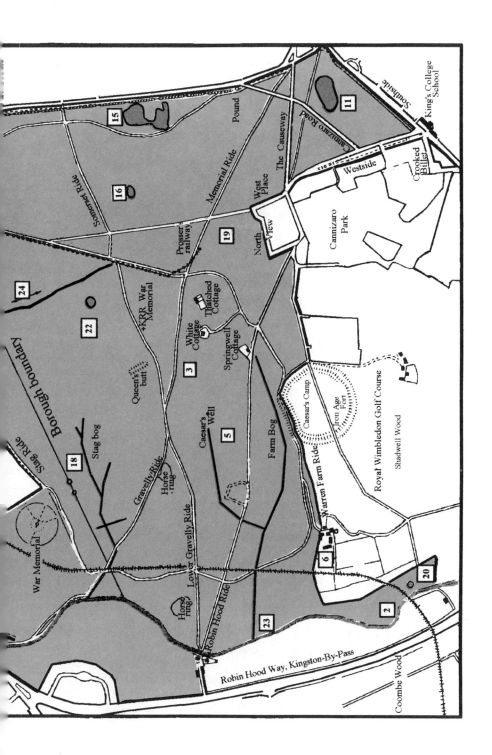

USING THE WATER SPLASH AT SEVEN POST POND c. 1908
(NOTE THE WIMBLEDON BUS IN THE BACKGROUND)

PONDS AND STREAMS

Most people know Beverley Brook and the three main ponds on Wimbledon Common: Kingsmere, Queensmere, and Rushmere, but there are several more in existence, as well as some that have disappeared altogether.

RUSHMERE
This pond dates back to Tudor times, when it was known as Rushmore, and possibly even earlier. Charters of A.D.693 and 957 mention the name, though it is not certain that it is the pond that is being referred to. In centuries gone by rushes from the pond were used for matting and for the roofs of the Village cottages.

QUEENSMERE
This came later, being artificially created in 1887 to commemorate Queen Victoria's Golden Jubilee. There has also long been a tradition of early morning bathing in Queensmere – for men only for some reason, and at one time there was even a diving board there. In 1984 the dead body of a Russian spy-hunter named Boris Hatton (formerly Baklanov) was found here. The circumstances surrounding his death were never established and the coroner recorded an open verdict.

KINGSMERE
Also artificially created around the same time as Queensmere, Kingsmere is now a haven for breeding coots, moorhens, Canada geese and mallards.

SEVEN-POST POND
Situated opposite the entrance to Inner Park Road on Parkside it takes its name from the posts fixed in the pond at one time to show water depth. This was essential up to the beginning of the 20th century for the many people who drove their horse-drawn carts and carriages through it. The 'water-splash' prevented the wooden wheels from becoming too dry and cracking (see picture opposite).

BLUEGATE GRAVEL PIT
Nearly opposite Calonne Road on Parkside it takes its name from the blue gates which once stood at the entrance to Lord Spencer's estate. As its name suggests, it was also, like some other ponds on the Common, a former gravel pit; the gravel being extracted for road-surfacing. It is not known when Bluegate became a pond, but it was still a gravel pit in 1821 when a tragedy occurred here. Two brothers, Edward and David Penner, and two friends died playing in the pit when they were buried in a fall of gravel. The boys' ages ranged from eight to thirteen.

HOOKHAMSLADE
An older pond just to the west of Bluegate. There is mention of the name Hookham Slade in the manor court rolls of 1763, though a pond is not specified. It may be that the area was known as Hookham Slade before a pond existed. Previous explanations of the name consider Slade as denoting a strip of greensward, but the Hookham part has remained a mystery. The pond was drained in 1911 to make space clear of heath for the coronation bonfire – a rather extreme undertaking with dire consequences for its indigenous wildlife. The pond is now happily flourishing again and has willow warblers breeding here each Spring. It is also home to a variety of dragonflies including the rare black darter and emerald damselfly.

Wimbledon Common, - Scio Pond.
(near Roehampton)

SCIO HOUSE AND POND c. 1910

JERRY'S POND

It is not easy to escape the legend of Wimbledon's most famous highwayman, Jerry Abershaw on Wimbledon Common, and here is a pond named after him. It is situated near the spot where Abershaw was gibbeted in 1795. At the turn of the 20th century there were two ponds here by Jerry's Hill, but today just one remains. It is named on some maps as the Curling pond after the sport that was regularly played here until as recently as just before the last war.

THE BLACK PONDS

Near the southern end of Stag Lane lie this pair of small ponds, sometimes known as the Silent Pools. Remote, and not easily accessible they support a variety of pond-life.

BUCKY'S POND

One of the lost ponds, with an intriguing name. Could Bucky have been perhaps a horse which regularly drank from its waters? The pond was situated at the edge of the Common by North View, and seems to have disappeared by the early 20th century.

FISHPONDS

These gave their name to Fishponds Wood which still exists between the Royal Wimbledon golf course and Beverley Brook. This area is thought to be ancient woodland and is now protected by the London Wildlife Trust. A very pretty and peaceful part of the Common which is little-known. One of the ponds is believed to be the original mill-pond which lay adjacent to the 15th century water-mill owned by Walter Cromwell. (In dry weather there is often just one, or even no ponds here).

SCIO POND

Situated near the junction of Roehampton Lane and the A3 this pond was named after nearby Scio House. The 18th century building was a residential home for a succession of upper middle-class families until 1924 when it became a hospital for ex-army officials. Despite local protests it was demolished in 1982. The unusual name of the house was bestowed on it by one of its 19th century residents, Eustratios C. Ralli, a Greek merchant who named it after the island of his birth.

RAVINE POND

A man-made pond which has been created recently. Just near Inner Windmill Road, it started with the name Millennium pond when it was created in 1997 and the name was changed in 1999. Despite its newness it has already begun to attract wildlife, and newts, dragonflies, and frogs' spawn have been seen.

BEVERLEY BROOK

The brook enters Wimbledon Common from Richmond Park near the Robin Hood gate and meanders down along the west side, leaving at the extreme south-west corner by the playing fields at Beverley Avenue. The name is believed to derive from the fact that the area was once populated by beavers, probably in Saxon times.

It would seem too that at one time the Beverley was more than the modest stream that exists now. In the 15th century a water-mill was working here which would have needed stronger waters to drive it. The location is still marked on maps as Mill Corner.

Early Morning Bathing. Queensmere. Wimbledon Common

Reeves

EARLY MORNING BATHERS AT QUEENSMERE c. 1920

THE RAVINE

The Ravine is the small stream running from Ravine pond to Queensmere. Today it is little more than a trickle of water but a century ago it was rather healthier. Walter Johnson's map of 1912 shows it reaching from Queensmere almost to Hookhamslade, though unfortunately it is wrongly named as Glen Albyn. This is actually a smaller stream running parallel to Willows Ride to the north of the windmill.

GLEN ALBYN

The name was probably bestowed on it by the London Scottish regiment who founded the golf club at the Windmill in the 19th century. The original Glen Albyn is a massive 30 mile ravine stretching along the banks of Loch Ness and Loch Lochy. An ironic dig then by the Scottish soldiers who found this tiny gully near their HQ on Wimbledon Common.

OTHER STREAMS

There are other small fingers of water to found on the Common, notably near Stag bog and Farm bog, but these have never been named.

Walkers on Wimbledon Common on November 20th 1964 would no doubt have been astonished to see Beatle John Lennon wandering around reading his own poems aloud, accompanied by Dudley Moore! He was there filming a segment for the Peter Cook and Dudley Moore television series *Not Only But Also*, and read his comic poem *Deaf Ted, Danoota, (And Me)* while walking between the windmill and Queensmere. The film was broadcast on BBC1 on January 9th 1965.

WILDLIFE

Despite its urban setting and intensive use by walkers, golfers, horse-riders and cyclists the Common still plays host to a large number of birds, animals and insects.

There are five species of bat alone, as well as rabbits, foxes, weasels, lizards, frogs, toads, voles, and field mice. There have even been recent reports of a muntjac deer finding its way on to the Common.

Of course, many animals that once thrived here have now gone. The natterjack toad, the shrew and the stoat have all disappeared within living memory. Going back to the beginning of the 20th century one would also have found the red squirrel and the hare. There was even a herd of cows roaming the Common in those days.

There may have been beavers here in Saxon times which gave their name to Beverley Brook. And was the 17th century Baldfaced Stag inn named after the animal appearing locally? We know that there were deer on the Common around that time as a warrant issued in 1636 informed the King that roe deer had been escaping from the Old Park at Wimbledon (now the area between Westside and Beverley Brook).

Today the Common has a depleted but still large variety of birds making their home here, as well as several visiting species. Partridge and pheasant, among others are no longer seen, but woodpeckers are not uncommon. Others that can be spotted include sparrowhawk, owl, nuthatch, chiffchaff, and various varieties of tit. Visiting birds include the cuckoo, whinchat and redpoll.

The Common is also one of London's best places to see dragonflies and damselflies – usually around the ponds. There are over a dozen different species including hawkers, darters, skimmers, and the blue damselfly. The Common also plays host to two dozen species of butterfly including the white-letter hairstreak which is not often seen in the capital.

There is an abundance of plant life to be found on the Common too: gorse, bluebells, many varieties of grass, blackberries, raspberries, bracken, bramble and holly. The flora varies depending on which part of the Common is visited but there is plenty to see, especially away from the main paths and buildings.

There are figwort, forget-me-not, and foxgloves, honeysuckle, hawthorn, and heather, bush vetch, star sedge, and marsh bedstraw. There is bur-reed, crack willow, and bugle, cuckoo flower, blackthorn, and gypsywort – the list of wonderful names goes on, but why not see for yourself?

Trees on the Common include oak, beech, yew, sycamore, lime, ash, silver birch, willow, and elder.

So there is much to discover and enjoy, perhaps far more than many people realise.

POETS AND WRITERS

It is surprising how many writers and poets have lived within walking distance of the Common, including several who wrote about it.

In the 19th century Leigh Hunt rhapsodised about the Common. He spoke of the furze as a 'golden undulation, a foreground, and from some points of view a middle distance fit to make the richest painter despair: a veritable Field of Cloth of Gold.... The gold goes stretching away into the distance towards the dark trees, like the rich evening of a poetic life.' He invited literary friends such as W.M. Thackeray to dine with him at the Rose and Crown in the Village and to walk on the Common. Thackeray was impressed too and described the Common as 'noble' and the air and green country as 'delightfully fresh'.

Later that century, the poet Algernon Swinburne strolled daily across the Common from his Putney home to the Rose and Crown. Perhaps it was for the pleasant walk, as another of his haunts was the much nearer Green Man on Putney Heath.

Swinburne's house, the Pines, was shared by fellow writer Walter Theodore Watts-Dunton who also enjoyed walking on the Common and Heath. He too was often accompanied by literary friends such as George Borrow, chronicler of gypsy life and author of *Romany Rye*.

Borrow also visited another literary friend at Putney, the poet Dr. Gordon Hale. Watts-Dunton recalled the three of them strolling to Richmond Park and stopping at the Baldfaced Stag in Portsmouth Road to view highwayman Jerry Abershaw's sword which was still there a century after his execution.

In the 20th century Lord Baden-Powell wrote his *Scouting For Boys* at the windmill on the Common in 1902, and in 1976 the then Poet Laureate Sir John Betjeman wrote a short poem about the windmill. *The Old Surrey Working Woman* was written especially for the restoration appeal.

Wimbledon author Captain Marryat also immortalised the Common in his novel *Jacob Faithful* when the eponymous hero goes shooting there. He and his friend get lost in a snowstorm and are startled by the sound of the remains of Jerry Abershaw's corpse swinging on the gibbet (three years after his demise).

Other writers who have lived near the Common and who no doubt used it recreationally were John Galsworthy, who lived at Coombe, Edward Gibbon, who was born at Lime Grove in Putney Hill, Robert Graves who was born in Lauriston Road, W.T. Stead who lived in Church Road and novelist Margaret Oliphant who lived at the Hermitage in West Place (novelist Hall Caine also once lived at this address). Also living nearby in the 19th century were John Morley, Theodore Hook (creator of *John Bull* magazine), and Douglas Jerrold. In addition to this there were many other writers who visited the area frequently. Lewis Carroll for example, had an uncle living in Putney and was a regular visitor.

In modern times the Common continues to be a source of inspiration for writers from Wombles creator Elizabeth Beresford to the comic novelist Nigel Williams.

THE GREEN MAN AT PUTNEY HEATH c. 1905

PUBLIC HOUSES

Wimbledon Common and Putney Heath have been well served with pubs over the centuries and even today there are more than half a dozen of them left. The pubs and inns were until quite recently the main focal points of leisure time for many and important places for travellers to stop. From the coaching days right through to the present their history and that of the Common are closely inter-linked. The stories of a select few follow:

THE GREEN MAN
Old pubs attract legends as old ships attract barnacles, and like barnacles they are notoriously difficult to remove once attached. The Green Man is no exception to this unwritten law. It is rumoured to have been built on the site of the smithy once owned by Walter Cromwell, father of Thomas Cromwell, and there are tales of Dick Turpin hiding his pistols here. So what is the real story of the Green Man?

It dates back to around 1700, but the idea that it is built on the site of Walter Cromwell's house and smithy seems to be wrong. The location of Cromwell's dwelling was said to be 'on the highway from Richmond to Wandsworth' at the sign of the Anchor. This would place it on the Upper Richmond Road where there was indeed an Anchor inn, which today is known as the Fox & Hounds.

And what of Dick Turpin? He undoubtedly varied his hunting grounds for highway robbery victims and did turn his attentions south of the river, but why he should have hidden his pistols at the Green Man, and whether he ever did we shall never know. What was described as a 'horse pistol' was found at the inn around 1800, but this was thought to be a relic of the duels that were fought nearby around that time.

However, it is known that two 18th century footpads, Witlock and Brown, frequented the Green Man among other local inns. It was their custom to haunt such places and waylay wealthy-looking victims as they left, perhaps slightly the worse for drink. As with so many of their kind they were eventually hanged at Tyburn (in 1773).

A more modern villain associated with this public house is Great Train Robber Bruce Reynolds. He had lived in Putney from birth, moved away as a child, and returned in adulthood. In his autobiography he recalls taking Sunday walks to the Green Man for a pint of Young's best bitter just prior to the train robbery.

After the robbery Reynolds moved from Putney to Queensway, and after that to Wimbledon. There have long been tales of the train robbery gang meeting in the Swan in the Ridgway, so it seems that this is not beyond the bounds of possibility. Another member of the gang, Gordon Goody, was also living in Putney with his mother just before the Great Train Robbery. Goody, incidentally, was known by the other gang members as 'The Footpad' – an echo of those other local villains Witlock and Brown.

The Green Man has other claims to fame too. It was, along with the Rose and Crown in Wimbledon Village, a favourite haunt of the poet Swinburne. Also, in the first world war it was the summer headquarters of the 8th battalion of Surrey Volunteers whose orderly room adjoined the inn. The pub had been leased by Young's brewery since 1831 and the freehold was bought by them exactly a century later.

VIEW FROM WIMBLEDON COMMON TO BALDFACED STAG
BUILDINGS TO LEFT OF NEWLANDS FARM c. 1910

Today the pub retains a village inn atmosphere and is a welcome stopping point for thirsty travellers walking the Heath. It is also probably the only pub in London where you can still play the ancient game of Ringing the Bull – a game similar to quoits which some believe dates back to Roman times.

BALDFACED STAG

This inn, now sadly gone, was one of the most interesting on the Common. Situated at the corner of Kingston Vale and Stag Lane, it had been there since around 1650. Over a century later it became the headquarters of a gang of highwaymen led by Jerry Abershaw. Its remote location also made it a favourite with crowds attending illegal prize-fights in the late 18th and early 19th centuries, as well as with duellists who used the area now covered by Queensmere pond.

The inn was a stopping point for noblemen and women travelling from London to Hampton Court Palace. It is even said that there was once an underground tunnel leading from the inn to one of Charles II's shooting boxes in Richmond Park.

By the 20th century the Baldfaced Stag had ceased to be an inn and had been taken over as a workshop by racing driver Kenelm Lee Guinness. Racing cars built here included the Golden Arrow with which Major Sir Henry Segrave broke the world land speed record at Dayton Beach, and Malcolm Campbell's Bluebird which set a new land speed record at Pendine Sands in 1924.

The old Baldfaced Stag building was finally demolished in 1937, symbolically the same year that Kenlem Lee Guinness died.

TELEGRAPH

The Telegraph had been a beer shop since 1856, and perhaps even earlier, but on March 30th 1861 an inn licence was applied for, stables were later built, and one James Wigley became its first innkeeper. The inn was of course named after the Admiralty telegraph that stood nearby. It had been there since 1796 and was originally a shutter station – a large frame with six shutters. This was replaced in 1822 with a mast and two 'arms'. Perhaps the inn's original name, the Telegraph Arms, was an intentional pun.

The telegraph had been set up to convey messages between London and Portsmouth at a time when fears of a Napoleonic attack were rife. The chain of telegraph stations started with the Admiralty, then continued at Chelsea, Putney, Kingston Hill, Cooper Hill and so on down to Portsmouth. (The last remaining link in the chain is the semaphore tower at Chatley Heath in Surrey which has been restored and is open to the public).

The telegraph survived until 1847 by which time electronic systems, invented in 1838, were being used. The electronic telegraph of course did not have the same drawbacks to face as the shutter system - such as fog.

Note: For more information about the Baldfaced Stag see *Pubs of Wimbledon Village* by this author.

CHARGE OF HUSSARS AND LANCERS 1860

Sometimes, messages would be received at Putney from Portsmouth, but because of the London fog they could not be transmitted to Chelsea. On these occasions, one of the operators would have to run from Putney to Chelsea and deliver the message personally. For this he would be paid a shilling.

When the telegraph station finally closed on December 31st 1847 its last superintendent was Lieutenant Lardner Dennys – a veteran of the Battle of Trafalgar. He and his family were allowed to stay on at the telegraph station for a year until he found an alternative situation. It has been suggested that it may have been he who started the beer shop, but this has not been substantiated.

Today the name of the inn keeps alive the memory of the telegraph station and the pub itself is a popular attraction despite being tucked away in the middle of Putney Heath. Until recently it was known for the giant chessboard outside with its four-foot high pieces, but these unfortunately have not been kept at the pub since the late 1990s.

OTHERS

Also around the Common are the Hand in Hand, Crooked Billet, Fox and Grapes, and Rose and Crown. In addition to these there was once also the Rising Sun which closed two centuries ago. Details on all these have been covered in *Pubs of Wimbledon Village (Past & Present)* by this author. One more modern pub near Putney Heath also has a name inspired by the Common: The Ranger. And another modern pub, the Highwayman in Petersfield Rise just off Roehampton Lane is named after Jerry Abershaw.

A recent London pub guide informs us of the World War II bomber pilot who after crashing on the Common, staggered into the Fox and Grapes for a stiff drink. Sadly, this was not possible as the German pilot and crew of three all died in the crash. It took place in the early hours of Friday May 9th 1941 when the plane crashed on the first fairway of the Royal Wimbledon golf course. The incendiary bombs it was carrying exploded, lighting up the night sky and sending whitish-blue balls of fire hundreds of feet into the air, which were described by one witness as being like the effect of a giant Roman candle. One member of the crew had made a last-minute attempt to bale out but was killed when he landed in a garden in nearby Wool Road.

The use of the Common by the National Rifle Association in the 19th century conjures up images of people shooting at targets, but the Common was also the venue for spectacular military displays and mock battles (see picture opposite). These battles which began in the early days of the NRA sometimes involved as many as 15,000 men – three times the entire population of Wimbledon at the time!

HORSE DRAWN TRAM AT AN A MEETING 1864

RAILWAYS AND TRAMS

Although not much trace can be seen today, there were once trains and trams running on Wimbledon Common, and there was even a proposal to run the District Line of the London Underground through the centre too.

The experimental railway of William Prosser ran in 1845 from the windmill to Thatched Cottage and today leaves us the long straight path connecting the two. Also, an aerial view of the Common still clearly shows the large turning circle north of the windmill. The railway never went beyond the experimental stage however and the innovations of wooden rails and guide wheels instead of flanges were never taken up.

The next form of transport came in 1864 when a tramway was set up to transport spectators to the National Rifle Association meetings. It ran from the pound at the south end of the Common and parallel with Parkside to just north of the windmill. Initially the trams were horse-drawn (see picture opposite), and by 1877 they were steam-driven. However, the NRA moved its event from Wimbledon to Bisley in 1889 following the accidental shooting of a gravedigger in Putney Vale cemetery, and again the Common was quiet.

But in 1881 a proposal was made to extend the District Line from Putney down through the middle of the Common to Kingston. Though this would have no doubt afforded an attractive view for the train passengers it would have irreparably shattered the peace of the Common. It seems incredible that this proposal was seriously considered, let alone almost carried out, especially since the Common had only just been saved by the conservators a mere four years previously. The proposed route (shown on the map in this book) would have passed through new stations at Tibbets Corner, Wimbledon Common (opposite Richmond Park's Robin Hood Gate), and Coombe. The section across Putney Heath and Wimbledon Common was originally going to be a covered way, and then was mooted to include a 1700-yard tunnel. But part of the route across the Common was still planned to be open and was to be shielded from the activities of the National Rifle Association who still met there.

But happily, the railway was not to traverse the Common. Although work had begun, with turf being cut at Coombe, the District Railway Company ran into financial difficulties and the alternative route through Wimbledon Park was financed by LWSR.

Since then the Common has returned to the quieter and time-honoured modes of transport such as walking and horseriding.

During the American war of 1812 Fort McHenry in Baltimore Harbour was being bombarded with rockets by the British fleet. These had been designed by Sir Richard Congreve who had reputedly tested them on Wimbledon Common. The sight of the bombs exploding in the air at Fort McHenry inspired Francis Scott Key to write the words which were to become the lyrics for the American national anthem. So the 'bombs bursting in the air' and the 'rocket's red glare' of the Star Spangled Banner had their origins on our Common.

KINGS & QUEENS

Apart from attracting the attentions of writers and artists over the centuries, the Common has not escaped the notice of royalty.

Queen Victoria opened the first National Rifle Association Meeting here in 1860, and two hundred years previously Charles II inspected his troops on Putney Heath in 1684.

George III reviewed his guards here in 1767, and the Surrey Volunteers in 1799. It was also George III who was used as a royal guinea pig when inventor David Hartley demonstrated his 'fireproof house' which had been built on Putney Heath in 1776. While the King, and Queen Charlotte took breakfast on the upper floor a fire blazed below them on the ground floor. Only some copper and iron sheets between the floors prevented regicide.

Adjoining Wimbledon Common in the 16th century was the Old Park which had been in the hands of Henry VIII from 1536 onwards. Taking up the area now covered by Cannizaro Park and the Royal Wimbledon golf course it was used by Charles I as a place to keep his roe deer while Richmond Park was being enclosed.

During the time of the Commonwealth 3000 men of Surrey met on Putney Heath to march to Parliament and petition for the restoration of Charles I. Unfortunately, once at their destination they were attacked by Cromwell's men and their leader, an unnamed miller from Wandsworth, was killed.

As mentioned elsewhere in this book, the Common seems to have been used by royalty for horseracing. Pepys records in 1667 that the King and Duke of York had gone to Putney Heath 'to run some horses'.

Other monarchs who would have seen the Common in past centuries include Elizabeth I. On one occasion the inhabitants of Wimbledon were charged 1s 8d each for regravelling of the roads prior to her travelling from Nonsuch palace to Putney.

In fact, with the road alongside the Common running from London to the coast many kings and queens would have used it. It has been said that Henry V travelled this road *en route* to Agincourt. Perhaps even some of the Saxon kings crowned at nearby Kingston would have been familiar with the road.

In modern times the Common has been used to celebrate royal occasions. As mentioned elsewhere in this book Queensmere was created in 1887 to commemorate Queen Victoria's golden jubilee and Hookhamslade pond was drained in 1911 for the coronation bonfire. In 1935 the silver jubilee of King George V and Queen Mary was celebrated on May 6th. A procession through the town ended at the Common, and the King's broadcast to the nation was played through loudspeakers prior to a grand fireworks display.

So the royal associations with the Common go back a long way and show how the Common has long been a preferred place for recreation and celebration alike.

END PIECE

This book has attempted to discover some new facts about the Common and to expand on some of its lesser-known history.

Facts and stories well covered in previous books such as those of the windmill, the National Rifle Association and duelling have been avoided unless something new could be added.

The Common continues to hold much mystery and there is undoubtedly plenty more to discover about the people who have lived and worked here and the ever-changing wildlife.

If the Common is a living entity it must inevitably become imbued with the imprint of the centuries of activity concentrated here, and it is impossible to walk the Common today without feeling a sense that one is surrounded by history.

One can almost hear the shouts of the crowds attending prize-fights, the massed gunfire of military reviews, the galloping horses of stagecoach days and beneath it all the gentle turn of the water-mill.

One can imagine the poets and artists strolling across the furze-covered heath and attempting to capture some of its glory. And as darkness descends, the ghosts and spirits of times past retread their earthly footsteps to the hooting of owls and the shrieking of foxes.

The Common is so much more than an expanse of grass and trees. As the surrounding town is modernised and rebuilt with almost reckless haste it is a historic continuum that in places almost seems to transcend time and change.

ACKNOWLEDGEMENTS

Ruth Murphy
Alan Elliot
Connie Curry
David Haldane
J. Wilbur Cocke
Norman Plastow
Dorian Gerhold
Surrey Record Office
Merton Local Studies Centre
Wandsworth Local History Library
The Wimbledon Society
Lady Helen Sheen
Special thanks to Cyril Maidment for drawing the map of the Common

PHOTOGRAPHS/PICTURES

Houses at Putney Heath by John Constable – V&A Picture Library
Coombe Wood by J. Constable – Yale Center for British Art, Paul Mellon Collection
A Horrible Creuel and Bloudy Murther Committed at Putney in Surrey, 1614
Shelfmark = 4° G 29.Art. – Bodleian Library, University of Oxford
Gypsy Camp – Illustrated London News
Mock Battle – Illustrated London News
NRA tram – Illustrated London News
Photographs from author's own collection

SELECT BIBLIOGRAPHY

Wimbledon Common – Walter Johnson
A History of Wimbledon and Putney Commons – edited by Norman Plastow
Putney and Roehampton Past – Dorian Gerhold
Greater London - Edward Walford
Wimbledon and Merton Annuals 1903, 1904, 1905, 1910
Prizefighting – John Ford
Memories of My Side of the Common – Connie Curry
The Romance of the Putney Telegraph – John Skelly
Memories of a Wimbledon Childhood– Patrick Fawcett
Historic Wimbledon – Richard Milward
Wimbledon's Railways – Alan Elliot
Nature Conservation in Merton – London Ecology Unit
Notes on John Constable – Peter Gerhold
A Long Time Gone – Chris Pitt
Pubs of Wimbledon Village – Clive Whichelow
More Mysterious Wimbledon – Ruth Murphy & Clive Whichelow

For more information on our publications and local walks visit our website at www.enigmapublishing.co.uk